LEAD YOUR AI AGENTS LIKE YOUR LIFE DEPENDS ON IT

Kurt Klintsson

CONTENTS

PROLOGUE

I have worked as a soldier, with soldiers, and commanded soldiers for nearly 20 years. I have faced questions that I did not understand, and I have asked questions that others did not comprehend. I have had to make the best of the resources available to me. However, success has often come when the questions have been asked correctly. When my superior looks me in the eyes and, with just a glance, knows that I have understood.

In some cases, one must learn to fly by the seat of their pants, but it certainly helps if the organization you are part of has a clear method of communication. An AI agent is a qualified assistant equipped with tools to solve a task. This is not entirely unlike a soldier.

When this book is published, the majority of the population will not have access to AI agents; instead, this capability will be owned by consultants who optimize businesses. However, as soon as AI agents are packaged in user-friendly interfaces that can be used in everyday life, they will swarm around everything and every operation. So how do you prepare your company for this? How should you think to ensure that your leadership can reach both your human assets and your AI agents, ultimately getting them to work together?

If you ask foolish questions, you will receive foolish answers. Garbage in, garbage out, as we say in the military. That is where we are now. In this book, I have broken down the leadership principles I have fortified during my 20 years of service and implemented them into a forty-page business model where you, as a leader, are expected to be ready to step into the next generation of entrepreneurship. And even though it may be hard to believe, we are already there.

This is not intended to be a handbook on leadership; rather, I aim to shed light on the reality as I perceive it, which has helped me in my career. I share insights and messages that I wish someone had given me earlier in my journey.In the civilian world, decisions may not directly impact life and death, but they will affect the lives of all your employees. Incorrect decisions create ripples that can extend far beyond the initial choice. An old truth about decision-making is that every decision has both positive outcomes and negative consequences. You must always identify these consequences, as that is where you determine whether the decision is worth implementing or not. Leadership is your sharpest weapon for wielding the sword of management in the most dangerous way. Be dangerous to your enemies, be caring towards your closest allies, and find out what they excel at, then utilize them accordingly.

"If you lose physical contact with the horse,
you lose control over the horse."

This page is dedicated to all of the heroes that didn't come home

AI - THE DUMBEST AND SMARTEST SOLDIER AT THE SAME TIME

I n the rapidly evolving landscape of future businesses, the integration of artificial intelligence (AI) presents a paradoxical challenge for leaders. AI can be likened to a soldier, embodying both extraordinary capabilities and significant limitations. This chapter explores this duality, highlighting how AI can excel in specific tasks while struggling with broader understanding and adaptability in the business environment.

AI's brilliance shines in data analysis, enabling organizations to process vast amounts of information quickly and efficiently. For instance, AI systems can analyze market trends, customer behavior, and operational efficiencies, providing valuable insights that drive strategic decision-making. However, this brilliance is often context-dependent. Just as a soldier may excel in combat but falter in negotiations, AI can perform exceptionally well in structured tasks but may lack the nuanced understanding required in complex business scenarios.

The analogy of a soldier is particularly relevant when considering

AI's role in business leadership. While AI can optimize processes and enhance productivity, it may struggle with tasks that require emotional intelligence, creativity, and adaptability—qualities that are essential for effective leadership. For example, AI can streamline supply chain management but may not fully grasp the intricacies of team dynamics or the importance of fostering a positive workplace culture.

Military leadership principles emphasize the importance of recognizing the strengths and weaknesses of both human leaders and AI. Leaders must understand that while AI can enhance operational capabilities, it cannot replace the critical thinking and emotional intelligence that human leaders bring to the table (yet). The greatest danger lies in over-relying on AI without acknowledging its limitations. Human leaders must remain engaged, providing oversight and context to ensure that AI tools are used effectively and ethically within the organization.

In conclusion, as businesses increasingly harness the potential of AI, it is crucial to approach its integration with a clear understanding of its dual nature. By combining the strengths of AI with the insights and intuition of human leaders, organizations can create a more effective and ethical approach to business leadership, ensuring that technology serves to enhance human capabilities rather than replace them.

AI - The Dumbest and Smartest Soldier at the same time – key lessons

1. Embrace Duality: Recognize that specific agents have both strengths and weaknesses. Use this understanding to guide your decisions on when to rely on specific agents and when to engage human insight.

2. Context Matters: Always consider the context in which specific agents operate. Evaluate whether the task at hand requires human intuition or if it can be effectively handled by specific agents.

3. Continuous Learning: Stay informed about specific agent developments and their implications for your organization. Foster a culture of learning to adapt to new challenges.

THE RIGHT TOOL FOR THE RIGHT JOB

In the rapidly evolving landscape of future businesses, the integration of artificial intelligence (AI) presents both opportunities and challenges. This chapter focuses on the critical importance of matching AI capabilities with specific tasks and environments, debunking the notion of AI as a universal solution. The adage, 'Don't judge a fish by its ability to climb a tree,' serves as a poignant reminder of the necessity to evaluate the environment and select the right tool for the job.

AI excels in certain contexts, particularly in data analysis, automation, and predictive modeling. For instance, AI can process vast amounts of data to identify trends and patterns that would be impossible for humans to discern in a timely manner. However, it is essential to recognize that not all tasks are suited for AI intervention. While AI can enhance efficiency in structured environments, it may falter in scenarios that require human intuition, creativity, or emotional intelligence—qualities that are vital for effective leadership and decision-making.

The analogy of a fish and a tree highlights the importance of understanding the inherent strengths and limitations of AI. Just as a fish is designed to thrive in water, certain tasks are inherently suited for AI, while others may require the nuanced understanding and adaptability that only humans can provide. For example, AI can optimize supply chain logistics and automate routine tasks, but it may not be the best choice for roles that involve complex interpersonal dynamics, such as conflict resolution or team motivation.

Military leadership principles emphasize the need for strategic decision-making when selecting tools for specific tasks. Leaders must carefully assess the unique challenges they face and consider the strengths and weaknesses of AI in relation to those challenges. By evaluating the environment and the nature of the task, leaders can make informed decisions about when and how to deploy AI effectively, ensuring that it complements rather than replaces human insight.

In conclusion, as businesses increasingly integrate AI into their operations, it is essential to approach its implementation with a clear understanding of its capabilities and limitations. By matching the right tool to the right job, organizations can harness the full potential of AI while ensuring that human judgment and creativity remain at the forefront of decision-making. This balanced approach will not only enhance operational efficiency but also foster a culture of innovation and adaptability in the face of an ever-changing business landscape.

The Right Tool for the Right Job – key lessons

1. Assess Suitability: Before deploying specific agents, evaluate whether they are the right tool for the specific task. Consider the environment and the unique requirements of the situation.

2. Avoid One-Size-Fits-All: Understand that specific agents are not a universal solution. Tailor your approach based on the specific needs of each task and team.

3. Encourage Experimentation: Foster a culture where team members feel comfortable experimenting with specific agents to discover their best applications.

THE ART OF ASKING THE RIGHT QUESTIONS

In both military operations and the realm of artificial intelligence (AI), the ability to ask the right questions and formulate clear tasks is paramount for success. This chapter explores the significance of precise communication, emphasizing that poorly framed inquiries lead to inadequate responses, whether in human interactions or when engaging with AI agents. By applying military leadership principles, leaders can enhance their effectiveness in guiding teams and leveraging AI capabilities.

Asking the right questions is a skill that requires practice and intentionality. In military contexts, leaders are trained to formulate inquiries that elicit actionable intelligence and drive strategic decision-making. Similarly, in business and AI interactions, the quality of the questions posed directly influences the quality of the answers received. Vague or ambiguous questions can result in misunderstandings, misinterpretations, and ultimately, suboptimal outcomes.

For instance, consider a scenario where a leader asks an AI system, 'What do you think about our sales performance?' This question is open-ended and lacks specificity, making it difficult for the AI to provide a focused and relevant analysis. In contrast, a more precise question such as, 'Can you analyze the sales data from the last quarter and identify trends in customer purchasing behavior?' provides clear direction and context, enabling the AI to deliver actionable insights.

Moreover, the importance of clear task formulation cannot be overstated. When assigning tasks to team members or AI agents, leaders must articulate their expectations and objectives with clarity. Military leaders excel in this area, often employing the principle of 'mission command,' which emphasizes the need for clear intent and purpose in orders. This approach ensures that all team members understand their roles and the desired outcomes, fostering accountability and alignment.

In the context of AI, providing clear instructions is equally critical. When tasks are poorly defined or lack a clear purpose, AI systems may struggle to deliver the expected results. For example, if a leader instructs an AI to 'improve customer engagement,' without specifying the metrics or strategies to be employed, the AI may generate irrelevant or ineffective solutions. Conversely, a well-defined task such as, 'Develop a targeted marketing campaign to increase customer engagement by 20% over the next quarter,' sets a clear objective and allows the AI to operate effectively within defined parameters.

In conclusion, the art of asking the right questions and formulating clear tasks is essential for effective leadership in both military and AI contexts. By prioritizing precise communication and well-defined objectives, leaders can enhance their ability to guide teams and leverage AI capabilities. This approach not only improves operational efficiency but also fosters a culture of clarity and accountability, ensuring that both human and AI agents work towards common goals.

The Art of Asking the Right Questions - Key Lessons

1. Precision in Questions: The quality of the questions asked directly influences the quality of the answers received; specific and clear inquiries lead to actionable insights.

2. Clear Task Formulation: Articulating expectations and objectives with clarity is essential for effective leadership, ensuring that both human and AI agents understand their roles and desired outcomes.

3. Mission Command Principle: Employing the principle of 'mission command' fosters accountability and alignment, enabling leaders to provide clear intent and purpose in their directives.

EVERYONE BENEFITS FROM DECISION-MAKING

In the complex landscape of modern business, effective decision-making is crucial for success. This chapter explores the benefits of both humans and AI agents participating in decision-making processes, highlighting how their collaboration can lead to more informed and effective outcomes. By combining human judgment and intuition with AI's ability to process vast amounts of data and identify patterns, organizations can create a synergistic approach to decision-making that enhances overall performance.

Human decision-makers bring invaluable qualities to the table, including emotional intelligence, creativity, and contextual understanding. These attributes allow humans to navigate complex social dynamics, consider ethical implications, and make nuanced judgments that AI may struggle to replicate. For instance, in situations that require empathy or moral reasoning, human leaders are essential for guiding teams and fostering a positive organizational culture.

On the other hand, AI agents excel in processing large datasets quickly and efficiently. They can analyze trends, forecast outcomes, and provide insights that would be impossible for humans to discern in a timely manner. By leveraging machine learning algorithms, AI can identify patterns and correlations within data that inform strategic decisions. This capability is particularly valuable in environments characterized by rapid change and uncertainty, where timely and data-driven decisions are critical.

The collaboration between humans and AI agents fosters mutual development and understanding. As AI systems learn from human input and feedback, they become better equipped to assist in decision-making processes. Conversely, human leaders can enhance their decision-making capabilities by utilizing AI-generated insights, leading to more informed choices. This dynamic relationship encourages continuous improvement and adaptation, ensuring that both humans and AI agents evolve together in response to changing business landscapes.

Military leadership principles emphasize the importance of teamwork and collaboration, which are equally applicable in the context of human-AI partnerships. Leaders must cultivate an environment where both human intuition and AI capabilities are valued and integrated into the decision-making process. By promoting open communication and collaboration, organizations can harness the strengths of both parties, leading to more effective and ethical decision-making.

In conclusion, the integration of AI agents into decision-making processes offers significant benefits for organizations. By recognizing the unique contributions of both humans and AI, businesses can foster a collaborative environment that enhances decision-making capabilities. This balanced approach not only improves operational efficiency but also promotes a culture of innovation and adaptability, positioning organizations for success in an increasingly complex and data-driven world.

Everyone Benefits from Decision-Making – key lessons

1. Value Human Insight: Always prioritize human judgment in decision-making processes, especially in areas requiring empathy and ethical considerations.

2. Leverage Specific Agent Insights: Use specific agent-generated data to inform your decisions, but do not let it replace your critical thinking.

3. Foster Collaboration: Encourage open communication between human and specific agents to enhance decision-making outcomes.

RECOGNIZING THE LIMITS OF AI

In the rapidly evolving landscape of technology, it is essential to recognize the limitations of artificial intelligence (AI). This chapter delves into the inherent constraints of AI, acknowledging its inability to perform certain tasks that require human ingenuity, creativity, and emotional intelligence. By understanding when AI can be a valuable tool and when it falls short, organizations can make informed decisions about its deployment, ensuring that both human and AI intelligence are utilized effectively.

AI excels in processing large datasets, identifying patterns, and automating routine tasks. However, it struggles in areas that demand creativity, critical thinking, and the ability to navigate complex social dynamics. For instance, while AI can generate reports based on data analysis, it may lack the ability to craft a compelling narrative or develop innovative solutions to unprecedented challenges. Tasks that require out-of-the-box thinking, such as product design or strategic planning, often necessitate the unique insights that only human intelligence can provide.

Military leadership principles emphasize the importance of understanding the strengths and weaknesses of both human and AI agents. Just as military leaders must recognize when to rely on their troops' intuition and experience, business leaders must understand when to engage human creativity and judgment over AI capabilities. This discernment is crucial in ensuring that organizations do not over-rely on AI, which can lead to a false sense of security and potentially detrimental outcomes.

Moreover, the collaboration between humans and AI should be viewed as a partnership rather than a replacement. While AI can enhance operational efficiency, it cannot replicate the nuanced understanding that human leaders bring to the table. For example, in high-stakes situations where ethical considerations are paramount, human judgment is irreplaceable. Military leaders often face complex moral dilemmas that require a deep understanding of context, values, and human emotions—areas where AI falls short.

In conclusion, recognizing the limits of AI is essential for effective leadership in any organization. By understanding when AI can serve as a valuable tool and when it is necessary to rely on human intelligence, leaders can create a balanced approach that leverages the strengths of both. This understanding not only enhances decision-making but also fosters a culture of innovation and adaptability, ensuring that organizations remain resilient in the face of challenges.

Recognizing the Limits of Specific Agents – key lessons

1. Know the Boundaries: Understand the limitations of specific agents and recognize when human creativity and ingenuity are necessary.

2. Promote Human-Specific Agent Collaboration: Create opportunities for specific agents to assist humans rather than replace them, ensuring that both can contribute their strengths.

3. Ethical Awareness: Always consider the ethical implications of specific agent deployment and ensure that human values guide decision-making.

SETTING THE
RIGHT COURSE

In the ever-evolving landscape of business, the integration of artificial intelligence (AI) presents both opportunities and challenges. This chapter introduces the concept of using military principles to guide the implementation and management of AI within a company. By drawing parallels between military operations and AI deployment, organizations can leverage proven strategies to enhance their effectiveness and achieve their objectives.

One of the fundamental tenets of military leadership is the establishment of clear goals. Just as military operations require a well-defined mission to succeed, AI initiatives must begin with specific, measurable objectives. These goals provide a roadmap for the deployment of AI technologies, ensuring that all efforts are aligned with the organization's overall strategy. By setting clear expectations, companies can better assess the impact of AI on their operations and make necessary adjustments along the way.

Strategy is another critical component of successful military operations, and it plays a vital role in AI implementation as well. Military leaders develop comprehensive strategies that consider the unique challenges of the battlefield, and similarly, business leaders must craft strategies that account for the complexities of integrating AI into their operations. This involves understanding the capabilities and limitations of AI, as well as the specific needs of the organization. A well-thought-out strategy enables companies to prioritize their AI initiatives, allocate resources effectively, and mitigate potential risks.

Execution is where the plans come to life, and this is where military principles can provide valuable insights for AI deployment. In military operations, effective execution requires coordination, communication, and adaptability. These same principles apply to the implementation of AI technologies. Organizations must foster a culture of collaboration, ensuring that teams work together seamlessly to integrate AI into their workflows. Additionally, leaders must remain flexible and responsive to changes in the environment, adjusting their approach as needed to ensure successful outcomes.

In conclusion, the integration of military principles into the management of AI can significantly enhance an organization's ability to navigate the complexities of this technology. By establishing clear goals, developing effective strategies, and executing plans with precision, companies can set the right course for their AI initiatives. This approach not only improves operational efficiency but also positions organizations for long-term success in an increasingly competitive landscape.

Setting the Right Course
– key lessons

1. Define Clear Goals: Establish specific, measurable objectives for specific agent initiatives to ensure alignment with organizational strategy.

2. Develop a Strategic Plan: Create a comprehensive strategy for specific agent implementation that considers both capabilities and limitations.

3. Communicate Effectively: Ensure that all team members understand the goals and strategies related to specific agent deployment.

THE DANGERS OF
BLIND TRUST

In an age where artificial intelligence (AI) is becoming increasingly integrated into decision-making processes, it is crucial to address the dangers of blind trust in these systems. This chapter emphasizes the importance of critical thinking and the need for human oversight, exploring the risks associated with relying solely on AI's recommendations and decisions.

Blind trust in AI can lead to a false sense of security, where organizations may overlook the inherent limitations of these technologies. While AI can process vast amounts of data and identify patterns with remarkable speed, it lacks the ability to understand context, nuance, and the moral implications of its decisions. This is particularly concerning in high-stakes situations, such as military operations, healthcare, and financial markets, where the consequences of errors can be catastrophic.

Philosophically, trust is a complex construct that involves not only confidence in the capabilities of a system but also an understanding of its limitations. Trusting AI without critical evaluation can result in a dangerous complacency, where human judgment is sidelined in favor of algorithmic recommendations. This is akin to a military leader who blindly follows orders without questioning their validity or considering the broader implications of those actions. Just as military leaders must weigh the advice of their commanders against their own experiences and insights, business leaders must critically assess AI outputs, ensuring that human judgment remains at the forefront of decision-making.

Moreover, the reliance on AI can create a dependency that undermines the development of critical thinking skills within organizations. When teams become accustomed to deferring to AI for answers, they may lose the ability to analyze situations independently and make informed decisions. This erosion of critical thinking can have long-term consequences, as organizations may find themselves ill-equipped to navigate challenges that require human ingenuity and creativity.

In conclusion, while AI offers significant advantages in data analysis and decision-making, it is essential to approach its use with caution. The dangers of blind trust highlight the need for a balanced approach that values both AI capabilities and human judgment. By fostering a culture of critical thinking and encouraging oversight, organizations can harness the power of AI while safeguarding against the risks of over-reliance. This balance not only enhances decision-making but also ensures that ethical considerations remain central to the process, ultimately leading to more responsible and effective outcomes.

The Dangers of Blind Trust – key lessons

1. Question Specific Agent Outputs: Always critically evaluate specific agent recommendations and decisions, considering the context and potential biases.

2. Maintain Human Oversight: Ensure that human judgment remains central to decision-making processes involving specific agents.

3. Cultivate Critical Thinking: Encourage team members to develop their analytical skills to complement specific agent capabilities.

STAYING CLOSE TO THE PROBLEM

In the realm of artificial intelligence (AI), the adage 'out of sight, out of mind' can lead to significant pitfalls. This chapter advocates for active engagement and close monitoring of AI's performance, emphasizing the critical importance of human oversight and intervention. In a world increasingly reliant on AI, leaders must remain vigilant and involved in the process to ensure proper execution and mitigate potential risks.

Military leadership teaches us that situational awareness is paramount. Just as commanders must stay attuned to the dynamics of the battlefield, business leaders must maintain a close watch on AI systems and their outputs. This engagement allows leaders to identify potential issues before they escalate, ensuring that AI operates within the intended parameters and aligns with organizational goals. By staying close to the problem, leaders can provide timely feedback and make necessary adjustments, fostering a culture of continuous improvement.

Moreover, the complexity of AI systems often means that unexpected challenges can arise. These challenges may stem from data biases, algorithmic errors, or shifts in the operational environment. Leaders who remain actively involved are better positioned to recognize these issues and intervene when necessary. This proactive approach not only enhances the effectiveness of AI but also reinforces the importance of human judgment in the decision-making process.

Philosophically, the relationship between humans and AI should be viewed as a partnership rather than a hierarchy. While AI can process information and generate insights at remarkable speeds, it lacks the contextual understanding and ethical considerations that human leaders bring to the table. By remaining engaged, leaders can ensure that AI serves as a tool to augment human capabilities rather than replace them. This partnership is essential for navigating the complexities of modern decision-making, where the stakes are often high and the consequences of errors can be severe.

In conclusion, staying close to the problem is vital for effective AI management. By actively engaging with AI systems and maintaining oversight, leaders can ensure that these technologies are deployed responsibly and effectively. This approach not only mitigates risks but also fosters a culture of collaboration between humans and AI, ultimately leading to better decision-making and more successful outcomes.

Staying Close to the Problem – key lessons

1. Engage Actively: Maintain close involvement with specific agent systems to monitor performance and provide timely feedback.

2. Foster Situational Awareness: Stay attuned to the dynamics of specific agent operations and be prepared to intervene when necessary.

3. Build a Partnership: View the relationship between humans and specific agents as a collaborative partnership rather than a hierarchical one.

BEYOND THE RESULT

In the fast-paced world of artificial intelligence (AI), it is easy to become fixated on immediate outcomes and short-term successes. However, this chapter highlights the importance of continuous learning and development, advocating for a broader perspective that prioritizes the growth of both human and AI capabilities. By focusing on long-term benefits through continuous improvement, organizations can foster a culture of innovation and resilience.

Military leadership emphasizes the value of training and development, recognizing that the battlefield is constantly evolving. Similarly, in the realm of AI, leaders must understand that technology and its applications are in a state of flux. Continuous learning is essential for both human agents and AI systems to adapt to new challenges and opportunities. For instance, while AI can analyze data and generate insights, it requires ongoing updates and training to remain effective in a changing environment. Leaders must invest in the development of AI capabilities, ensuring that these systems are equipped to handle emerging complexities.

Moreover, the development of human capabilities is equally critical. As organizations integrate AI into their operations, it is essential to cultivate a workforce that is skilled in leveraging these technologies. This involves not only technical training but also fostering critical thinking, creativity, and emotional intelligence among team members. By prioritizing the development of human skills, organizations can create a synergistic relationship between human and AI agents, enhancing overall performance.

The long-term benefits of continuous improvement extend

beyond immediate results. Organizations that embrace a culture of learning are better positioned to navigate uncertainties and adapt to changing circumstances. This proactive approach allows leaders to identify potential challenges before they escalate, ensuring that both human and AI capabilities are aligned with organizational goals.

In conclusion, moving beyond the result requires a commitment to continuous learning and development. By prioritizing the growth of both human and AI capabilities, leaders can foster a culture of innovation and resilience that drives long-term success. This approach not only enhances operational effectiveness but also prepares organizations to thrive in an increasingly complex and dynamic landscape.

Beyond the Result – key lessons

1. Prioritize Continuous Learning: Encourage ongoing education and training for both human and specific agent capabilities.

2. Embrace a Growth Mindset: Foster a culture that values experimentation and learning from failures.

3. Focus on Long-Term Goals: Look beyond immediate results and prioritize the development of sustainable capabilities.

UNDERSTANDING THE HUMAN ELEMENT

As organizations increasingly integrate artificial intelligence (AI) into their operations, it is essential to recognize the human dimension of this transformation. This chapter examines the importance of empathy, communication, and building trust with employees during AI implementation. By addressing potential anxieties surrounding AI's role in the workplace, leaders can foster an environment of understanding and acceptance.

AI can evoke a range of emotions among employees, from excitement about new possibilities to anxiety about job security and changes in work dynamics. Leaders must acknowledge these feelings and approach the implementation of AI with empathy. By understanding the concerns of their teams, leaders can create a supportive atmosphere that encourages open dialogue. This communication is vital for addressing misconceptions and providing clarity about AI's role in the organization.

Building trust is another critical component of successful AI implementation. Employees are more likely to embrace AI when they feel that their leaders are transparent about the technology's capabilities and limitations. Leaders should engage in honest conversations about how AI will impact their roles and the organization as a whole. This transparency not only alleviates fears but also empowers employees to see AI as a tool that can enhance their work rather than replace it.

Moreover, fostering a culture of collaboration between humans and AI is essential. Leaders should encourage employees to participate in the AI implementation process, seeking their input and feedback. This involvement not only helps to demystify AI but also allows employees to feel a sense of ownership over the technology. When employees see themselves as active participants in the integration of AI, they are more likely to embrace it and leverage its capabilities effectively. In conclusion, understanding the human element of AI implementation is crucial for success. By emphasizing empathy, communication, and trust-building, leaders can address potential anxieties and foster a culture of acceptance. This approach not only enhances the effectiveness of AI integration but also strengthens the overall organizational culture, paving the way for a more collaborative and innovative future.

Understanding the Human Element – key lessons

1. Practice Empathy: Acknowledge and address the emotional responses of employees regarding specific agent integration.

2. Foster Open Communication: Create channels for dialogue about specific agents' role and impact on the workplace.

3. Build Trust: Be transparent about specific agent capabilities and limitations to alleviate fears and build confidence.

SPECIFIC AGENTS AS TEAM MEMBERS

In the evolving landscape of modern organizations, artificial intelligence is increasingly being recognized not just as a tool, but as a valuable team member. This chapter explores how AI can be integrated into the company culture, emphasizing the importance of fostering collaboration between AI agents and human employees. By promoting mutual respect and recognizing the unique strengths of each, organizations can create a more cohesive and effective workforce.

AI possesses remarkable capabilities in data analysis, pattern recognition, and task automation, allowing it to complement human efforts in various ways. However, for AI to be truly effective as a team member, leaders must cultivate an environment that encourages collaboration. This involves creating opportunities for AI and human employees to work together on projects, leveraging the strengths of both parties to achieve common goals.

Leaders play a crucial role in facilitating this integration. They must communicate the value of AI to their teams, highlighting how it can enhance productivity and support decision-making processes. By framing AI as a partner rather than a competitor, leaders can alleviate fears and foster a culture of collaboration. This shift in perspective is essential for building trust and ensuring that employees feel comfortable working alongside AI.

Moreover, recognizing the unique strengths of both AI and human employees is vital. While AI excels in processing large volumes of data and performing repetitive tasks, human employees bring creativity, emotional intelligence, and contextual understanding to the table. By acknowledging these differences, organizations can create a balanced approach that maximizes the contributions of both AI and human team members.In conclusion, integrating AI into the company culture as a valuable team member requires intentional efforts from leaders. By fostering collaboration, promoting mutual respect, and recognizing the unique strengths of each, organizations can harness the full potential of AI while enhancing the overall effectiveness of their teams. This collaborative approach not only drives innovation but also prepares organizations to thrive in an increasingly complex and dynamic environment.

Specific Agents as Team Members

1. Promote Collaboration: Encourage teamwork between specific agents and human employees to leverage their respective strengths.

2. Frame Specific Agents as Partners: Communicate the value of specific agents as supportive tools rather than competitors.

3. Recognize Unique Strengths: Acknowledge the distinct contributions of both specific agents and human team members.

CULTIVATING
TRUST IN AI

As organizations increasingly rely on artificial intelligence (AI) to drive decision-making and operational efficiency, the challenge of building trust in AI becomes paramount. This chapter addresses the critical importance of transparency, accountability, and demonstrating AI's reliability and consistency over time. By fostering trust in AI, organizations can ensure its responsible deployment and maximize its potential benefits.

Transparency is a foundational element in cultivating trust. Organizations must be open about how AI systems operate, including the data they use, the algorithms that drive their decisions, and the potential biases that may exist. By providing clear explanations of AI processes, leaders can demystify the technology and alleviate concerns among employees and stakeholders. This transparency not only builds confidence but also encourages a culture of accountability, where AI systems are held to the same standards as human decision-makers.

Accountability is essential in ensuring that AI is deployed responsibly. Organizations should establish clear guidelines and frameworks for AI usage, outlining the roles and responsibilities of both AI systems and human operators. This includes defining the parameters within which AI can operate and ensuring that there are mechanisms for oversight and review. By holding AI accountable for its actions, organizations can reinforce trust and demonstrate their commitment to ethical practices.

Demonstrating AI's reliability and consistency over time is crucial for building confidence in its capabilities. Organizations should track and report on AI performance metrics, showcasing its effectiveness in achieving desired outcomes. Regular assessments and audits of AI systems can help identify areas for improvement and ensure that AI continues to meet organizational standards. By consistently delivering reliable results, AI can earn the trust of employees and stakeholders alike.

In conclusion, cultivating trust in AI is a multifaceted challenge that requires a commitment to transparency, accountability, and consistent performance. By prioritizing these elements, organizations can build confidence in AI's capabilities and ensure its responsible deployment. This trust not only enhances the effectiveness of AI but also strengthens the overall organizational culture, paving the way for a successful integration of technology and human expertise.

Cultivating Trust in Specific Agents – Key lessons

1. Ensure Transparency: Be open about how specific agent systems operate and the data they use.

2. Establish Accountability: Create guidelines for specific agent usage that define roles and responsibilities.

3. Monitor Performance: Regularly assess specific agent systems to ensure reliability and consistency.

BEYOND THE SPECIFICATIONS

In the realm of artificial intelligence (AI), establishing trust goes beyond mere performance metrics and specifications. This chapter delves into the nuanced aspects of trust, recognizing that AI's ability to operate within its defined parameters is not sufficient for building genuine trust with human counterparts. To foster meaningful relationships, AI must demonstrate qualities such as empathy, understanding, and adaptability.

While AI systems can excel in executing tasks and processing data, their effectiveness in human interactions often hinges on their ability to connect on a deeper level. Empathy, for instance, is a critical component in building trust. AI that can recognize and respond to human emotions—whether through natural language processing or sentiment analysis—can create a more engaging and supportive experience for users. By acknowledging the emotional context of interactions, AI can foster a sense of connection and understanding.

Understanding is another vital aspect of trust. AI must be designed to comprehend the nuances of human behavior and decision-making. This involves not only processing information but also interpreting the intent behind actions and words. Leaders should encourage the development of AI systems that prioritize contextual awareness, enabling them to respond appropriately to varying situations and user needs.

Adaptability is equally important in cultivating trust. AI must be capable of learning from experiences and adjusting its responses based on feedback. This dynamic capability allows AI to evolve alongside human counterparts, fostering a collaborative environment where both parties can thrive. Leaders should advocate for continuous improvement in AI systems, ensuring they remain responsive to the changing needs of users and the organization.

In conclusion, building trust in AI requires a shift in perspective from mere performance to the cultivation of genuine connections. By encouraging AI to demonstrate empathy, understanding, and adaptability, leaders can foster a more collaborative relationship between humans and technology. This approach not only enhances the effectiveness of AI but also strengthens the overall organizational culture, paving the way for a future where AI and humans work together harmoniously.

Beyond the Specifications
– key lessons

1. Encourage Empathy in Specific Agents: Advocate for the development of specific agents that can recognize and respond to human emotions.

2. Foster Understanding: Ensure specific agent systems are designed to comprehend the nuances of human behavior.

3. Promote Adaptability: Support continuous improvement in specific agent systems to enhance their responsiveness to user needs.

WHEN THE ENDS JUSTIFY THE MEANS

In the realm of military operations, the integration of artificial intelligence (AI) agents presents unique ethical considerations, particularly when faced with difficult choices and potentially controversial outcomes. This chapter tackles the complex interplay between achieving military objectives and upholding ethical principles, emphasizing the need for careful evaluation and responsible decision-making by leaders.

The phrase 'the ends justify the means' often arises in discussions about military ethics, especially in high-stakes environments where the pressure to achieve objectives can be intense. While the pursuit of mission success is paramount, it is crucial for military leaders to recognize that the methods employed to achieve these goals can have significant ethical implications. Leaders must navigate these dilemmas with a clear understanding of their values and the potential consequences of deploying AI agents in various scenarios.

One of the primary challenges in using AI agents is the potential for bias in decision-making processes. If not carefully designed and monitored, AI systems can perpetuate existing biases or create new ones, leading to unfair or harmful outcomes. Military leaders must prioritize ethical considerations in the development and deployment of AI agents, ensuring that these systems are transparent, accountable, and free from bias. This involves implementing robust oversight mechanisms and regularly auditing AI systems to identify and address any ethical concerns.

Moreover, the ethical implications of AI agents extend beyond bias. Leaders must also consider the impact of these systems on privacy, security, and the overall well-being of individuals and communities. Responsible decision-making requires a holistic approach that takes into account the potential risks and benefits of deploying AI agents in military operations. Engaging stakeholders, including soldiers and civilians, in discussions about ethical considerations can help military organizations make informed choices that align with their values and societal expectations.

In conclusion, the ethical considerations of using AI agents in military contexts are complex and multifaceted. Leaders must strike a balance between achieving operational goals and upholding ethical principles, ensuring that their decisions reflect a commitment to responsible practices. By fostering a culture of ethical awareness and accountability, military organizations can navigate the challenges of AI deployment while maintaining their integrity and trustworthiness.

When the Ends Justify the Means – key lessons

1. Evaluate Ethical Implications: Always consider the ethical consequences of specific agent deployment in decision-making.

2. Engage Stakeholders: Involve relevant parties in discussions about the ethical use of specific agents.

3. Prioritize Transparency: Be open about the methods and decisions made in specific agent deployment.

THE VALUE OF PATIENCE

In the rapidly evolving landscape of artificial intelligence (AI) in business, the value of patience and understanding cannot be overstated. This chapter advocates for a patient approach when working with AI agents, acknowledging their potential for errors and the necessity for ongoing refinement. Business leaders must recognize that the journey of integrating AI into their operations is not a sprint but a marathon, requiring a long-term perspective and commitment to continuous improvement.

AI agents, while powerful tools for enhancing efficiency and decision-making, are not infallible. They can make mistakes, misinterpret data, or fail to adapt to new business environments. Leaders must approach the development and deployment of AI with a mindset that embraces these challenges. Patience is essential in allowing AI systems to learn from their errors and improve over time. Just as military leaders train their personnel to adapt and grow, business leaders must invest in the iterative training and refinement of AI agents to enhance their performance and reliability.

Moreover, the business environment is inherently complex and dynamic. Leaders must understand that the integration of AI agents into their operations will involve a learning curve, both for the technology and the teams that interact with it. By fostering a culture of patience, leaders can create an environment where experimentation and learning are encouraged, allowing teams to explore innovative solutions without the fear of immediate failure.

Continuous learning is a cornerstone of effective leadership, and this principle applies equally to the development of AI agents. Leaders should prioritize ongoing education and training for both human operators and AI systems, ensuring that they remain adaptable and responsive to changing market conditions. This commitment to learning not only enhances the capabilities of AI agents but also strengthens the overall effectiveness of business operations.

In conclusion, the value of patience in working with AI agents is paramount. Business leaders must adopt a long-term perspective, recognizing that the path to successful AI integration is paved with challenges and opportunities for growth. By fostering a culture of patience and continuous improvement, organizations can harness the full potential of AI while maintaining operational integrity and effectiveness.

The Value of Patience – key lessons

1. Embrace a Long-Term Perspective: Recognize that specific agent integration is a gradual process requiring time and effort.

2. Foster a Culture of Learning: Encourage experimentation and learning from mistakes.

3. Invest in Continuous Improvement: Commit to ongoing training and refinement of specific agent systems.

BEYOND TECHNICAL PROFICIENCY

In the realm of artificial intelligence (AI) in business, technical proficiency is just the beginning. This chapter emphasizes the importance of developing AI agents that not only perform tasks but also understand the broader context in which they operate and communicate effectively with human counterparts. Military leadership principles can provide valuable insights into fostering these essential qualities in AI agents, ensuring they exceed mere technical competence.

AI agents must be designed to recognize and interpret the nuances of human interactions. This involves not only processing data but also understanding the intent behind actions and words. Just as military leaders prioritize clear communication and situational awareness, business leaders must ensure that AI agents are equipped to engage meaningfully with their teams and stakeholders. This capability is crucial for building trust and collaboration in a business environment.

Moreover, empathy and creativity are vital attributes that AI agents should strive to embody. Empathy allows AI to recognize and respond to human emotions, creating a more engaging and supportive experience for users. In military contexts, leaders often rely on their ability to connect with their teams on a personal level; similarly, AI agents that can demonstrate empathy will foster stronger relationships and enhance teamwork.

Creativity is another essential quality that AI agents must develop. While traditional AI systems excel at executing predefined tasks, the ability to think creatively and propose innovative solutions is what sets exceptional AI apart. Business leaders should encourage the development of AI systems that can generate new ideas and approaches, much like military leaders who adapt strategies based on evolving circumstances.

In conclusion, the journey toward developing AI agents that go beyond technical proficiency requires a commitment to understanding the broader context of their roles. By fostering qualities such as empathy, creativity, and effective communication, business leaders can ensure that AI agents become valuable partners in achieving organizational goals. Embracing military leadership principles in this process will enhance the effectiveness of AI agents and strengthen the overall business environment.

Beyond Technical Proficiency – key lessons

1. Promote Contextual Understanding: Ensure specific agent systems are designed to comprehend the broader context of their tasks.

2. Encourage Empathy and Creativity: Advocate for the development of specific agents that can engage meaningfully with humans.

3. Foster Effective Communication: Ensure specific agents can communicate clearly and effectively with human counterparts.

AI AND THE HUMAN EXPERIENCE

In today's rapidly evolving workplace, the integration of artificial intelligence (AI) has a profound impact on the human experience. This chapter examines how AI can contribute to a positive and enriching work environment while also addressing the potential anxieties and concerns that arise from its role in shaping human lives. By applying military leadership principles, business leaders can navigate these challenges effectively.

AI has the potential to enhance productivity, streamline processes, and provide valuable insights that empower employees. However, leaders must recognize that the introduction of AI can also lead to feelings of uncertainty and apprehension among team members. Just as military leaders prioritize the well-being of their personnel, business leaders must foster an environment where employees feel supported and valued in the face of technological change.

To create a positive work environment, leaders should actively engage with their teams, encouraging open dialogue about the role of AI in their daily tasks. This transparency helps demystify AI and alleviates fears by clarifying how AI can serve as a tool to augment human capabilities rather than replace them. By emphasizing collaboration between AI and human employees, leaders can cultivate a culture of trust and innovation.

Moreover, leaders should consider the ethical implications of AI deployment in the workplace. Military leaders are trained to make decisions that prioritize the welfare of their troops; similarly, business leaders must ensure that AI systems are designed and implemented with a focus on enhancing the human experience. This includes addressing concerns about job displacement, privacy, and the potential for bias in AI decision-making.

In conclusion, the impact of AI on the human experience in the workplace is significant and multifaceted. By leveraging military leadership principles, business leaders can create a work environment that embraces the benefits of AI while addressing the anxieties and concerns of their teams. T

his balanced approach will not only enhance productivity but also promote a culture of well-being and collaboration, ensuring that technology serves to enrich the human experience.

Specific Agents and the Human Experience – key lessons

1. Engage Employees: Actively involve team members in discussions about specific agents' role in the workplace.

2. Address Anxieties: Acknowledge and address concerns about specific agents' impact on job security and work dynamics.

3. Foster a Positive Culture: Create an environment where specific agents are seen as tools for enhancement rather than replacement.

THE POWER OF
OBSERVATION

In the realm of artificial intelligence (AI), the power of observation and critical thinking is paramount for effective leadership. This chapter highlights the importance of carefully analyzing AI's behavior, identifying patterns, and understanding its underlying motivations. By applying military leadership principles, leaders can make informed decisions and guide the development of AI systems that align with organizational objectives.

Observation is a fundamental skill that military leaders cultivate to assess situations accurately and respond effectively. Similarly, business leaders must develop a keen sense of observation when interacting with AI. This involves monitoring AI's outputs, understanding its decision-making processes, and recognizing any anomalies or unexpected behaviors. By doing so, leaders can gain valuable insights into how AI operates and identify areas for improvement.

Critical thinking plays a crucial role in this process. Leaders should not only observe AI's actions but also question the rationale behind them. What data is the AI using to make decisions? Are there biases present in its algorithms? By critically analyzing AI's behavior, leaders can uncover potential issues and address them proactively, ensuring that AI systems function optimally and ethically.

Moreover, understanding the motivations of AI is essential for effective leadership. While AI lacks emotions and intentions, its design and programming reflect the goals set by its developers. Leaders must recognize that AI operates within the parameters defined by human input. By understanding these motivations, leaders can better align AI's capabilities with the organization's mission and values.

In conclusion, the power of observation and critical thinking is vital for leaders interacting with AI. By applying military leadership principles, leaders can enhance their ability to analyze AI behavior, identify patterns, and understand underlying motivations. This proactive approach will not only improve AI performance but also ensure that its development aligns with the broader goals of the organization.

The Power of Observation
– key lessons

1. Develop Observation Skills: Cultivate a keen sense of observation when interacting with specific agents.

2. Question Specific Agent Behavior: Regularly analyze specific agent outputs and question the rationale behind them.

3. Understand Specific Agent Motivations: Recognize that specific agents operate within parameters defined by human input.

EMBRACING THE POWER OF SPECIFIC AGENTS

In the rapidly evolving landscape of technology, artificial intelligence (AI) stands out as a powerful tool that has the potential to enhance human capabilities and overcome limitations. This chapter emphasizes the importance of embracing AI as a catalyst for innovation, efficiency, and problem-solving, while also recognizing the critical role of human oversight and collaboration. By applying military leadership principles, leaders can effectively integrate AI into their organizations.

AI offers remarkable capabilities that can augment human performance in various domains. For instance, in military operations, AI can analyze vast amounts of data to provide actionable insights, enabling commanders to make informed decisions swiftly. Similarly, in business, AI can streamline processes, optimize resource allocation, and enhance customer experiences. Leaders must recognize that AI is not a replacement for human intelligence but rather a complement that can elevate performance to new heights.

However, the integration of AI into decision-making processes must be approached with caution. Military leaders understand the importance of maintaining situational awareness and ensuring that decisions are made with a comprehensive understanding of the context. In the same vein, business leaders must ensure that AI systems operate within ethical boundaries and align with organizational values. This requires ongoing human oversight to monitor AI outputs, assess their implications, and intervene when necessary.

Collaboration between AI and human team members is essential for maximizing the benefits of AI technology. Leaders should foster an environment where employees feel empowered to leverage AI tools in their work. This involves providing training and resources to help team members understand how to effectively use AI, as well as encouraging open communication about the challenges and opportunities that AI presents.

In conclusion, embracing the power of AI presents a unique opportunity for leaders to enhance human capabilities and drive innovation. By applying military leadership principles, leaders can effectively integrate AI into their organizations while ensuring that human oversight and collaboration remain at the forefront. This balanced approach will not only improve efficiency and problem-solving but also create a culture of trust and empowerment within the organization.

Embracing the Power of Specific Agents – key lessons

1. Recognize Specific Agents Potential: Embrace specific agents as tools for innovation and efficiency.

2. Ensure Human Oversight: Maintain human involvement in specific agent decision-making processes.

3. Foster Collaboration: Encourage teamwork between specific agents and human employees to maximize benefits.

THE FUTURE OF LEADERSHIP

In the age of artificial intelligence (AI), the nature of leadership is evolving rapidly. This chapter explores how AI can transform traditional leadership models, empowering leaders to focus on strategic thinking, creativity, and building relationships while leveraging AI's capabilities for execution and analysis. By applying military leadership principles, leaders can navigate this transformation effectively.

AI has the potential to enhance decision-making processes by providing leaders with data-driven insights and predictive analytics. This allows leaders to make informed choices that align with organizational goals and respond proactively to emerging challenges. However, as AI takes on more analytical tasks, leaders must shift their focus toward higher-level strategic thinking and creative problem-solving. Military leaders are trained to think critically and adapt to changing circumstances; similarly, business leaders must cultivate these skills to thrive in an AI-driven environment.

Moreover, the integration of AI into leadership practices emphasizes the importance of building strong relationships within teams. While AI can analyze data and optimize processes, it cannot replicate the human touch that fosters collaboration and trust. Leaders must prioritize interpersonal skills, emotional intelligence, and effective communication to create a positive work culture that embraces AI as a partner rather than a replacement.

As leaders leverage AI's capabilities for execution and analysis, they must also remain vigilant about the ethical implications of AI deployment. Military leaders understand the importance of ethical decision-making in complex situations; business leaders must similarly ensure that AI systems are used responsibly and transparently. This includes addressing concerns about bias, privacy, and the impact of AI on employee roles.

In conclusion, the future of leadership in the age of AI presents both opportunities and challenges. By embracing military leadership principles, leaders can transform traditional models to focus on strategic thinking, creativity, and relationship building while effectively leveraging AI's capabilities. This balanced approach will not only enhance organizational performance but also foster a culture of trust and innovation.

The Future of Leadership
– key lessons

1. Focus on Strategic Thinking: Prioritize higher-level thinking and creativity in leadership roles.

2. Build Strong Relationships: Emphasize the importance of interpersonal skills and emotional intelligence.

3. Stay Ethical: Remain vigilant about the ethical implications of specific agent deployment in leadership.

EPILOGUE

As we reach the conclusion of this journey together, I want to take a moment to reflect on the profound changes we face in the realm of leadership and artificial intelligence. The integration of AI into our workplaces is not merely a technological shift; it is a transformation that challenges us to rethink our roles as leaders and collaborators.

Throughout this book, we have explored the dual nature of AI —its remarkable capabilities and its inherent limitations. Just as a soldier must understand both the power of their weapon and the importance of their judgment, so too must we embrace the strengths of AI while remaining vigilant about its shortcomings. The key to success lies in our ability to foster a partnership between human insight and machine efficiency, ensuring that we leverage technology to enhance our decision-making rather than replace the invaluable human touch.

I extend my heartfelt gratitude to you, the reader, for embarking on this journey with me. Your willingness to engage with these ideas reflects a commitment to growth and innovation in your own leadership practice. Remember, the path to effective leadership in the age of AI is paved with continuous learning, empathy, and a willingness to adapt.

As you move forward, I encourage you to ask the right questions, embrace the duality of AI, and cultivate a culture of collaboration within your teams. Trust in your human assets, recognize their unique strengths, and empower them to thrive alongside AI. In doing so, you will not only navigate the complexities of this new landscape but also inspire those around you to embrace the future with confidence.

In closing, let us remember that while technology may evolve, the essence of leadership remains rooted in our ability to connect, understand, and uplift one another. As we step into this new era, may we do so with courage, wisdom, and an unwavering commitment to the human experience. Thank you for reading and for being a part of this journey.

"The horse is not stupid; it just doesn't understand"

www.ingramcontent.com/pod-product-compliance
Lightning Source LLC
Chambersburg PA
CBHW070136230526
45472CB00004B/1559